Amazing Owls Coloring Book

This book is belongs to

_____

Panista Publishing

COLOR TEST PAGE

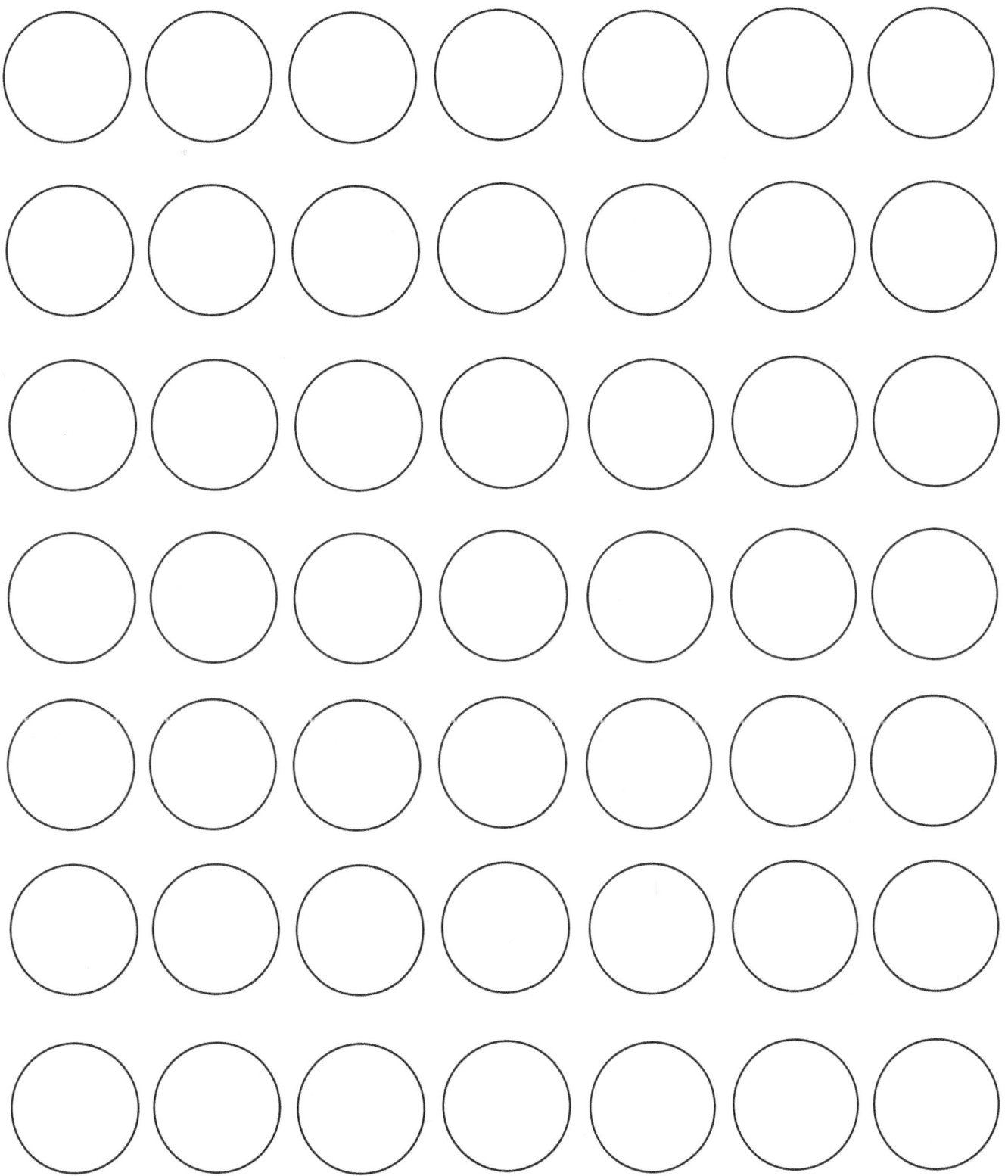

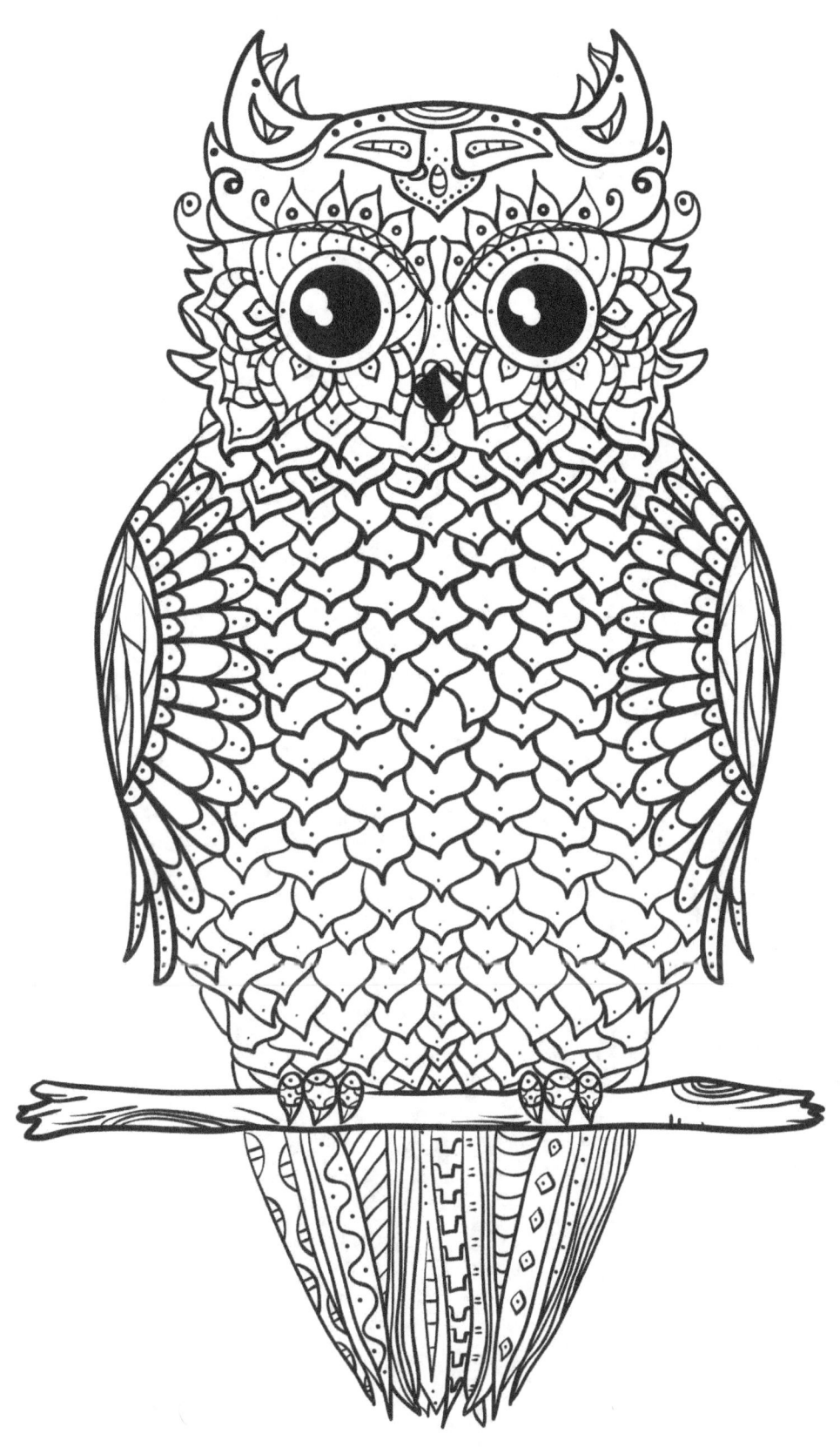

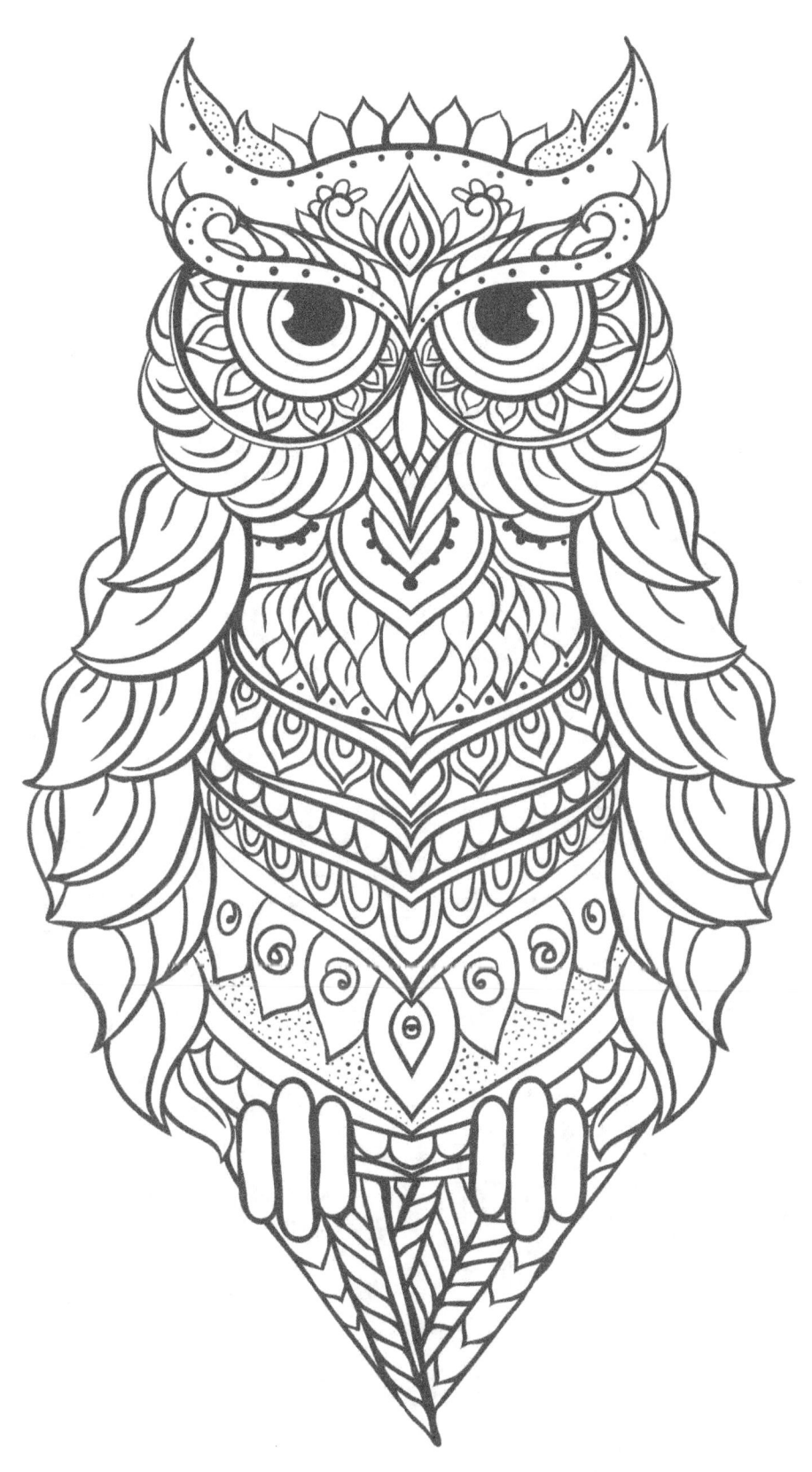

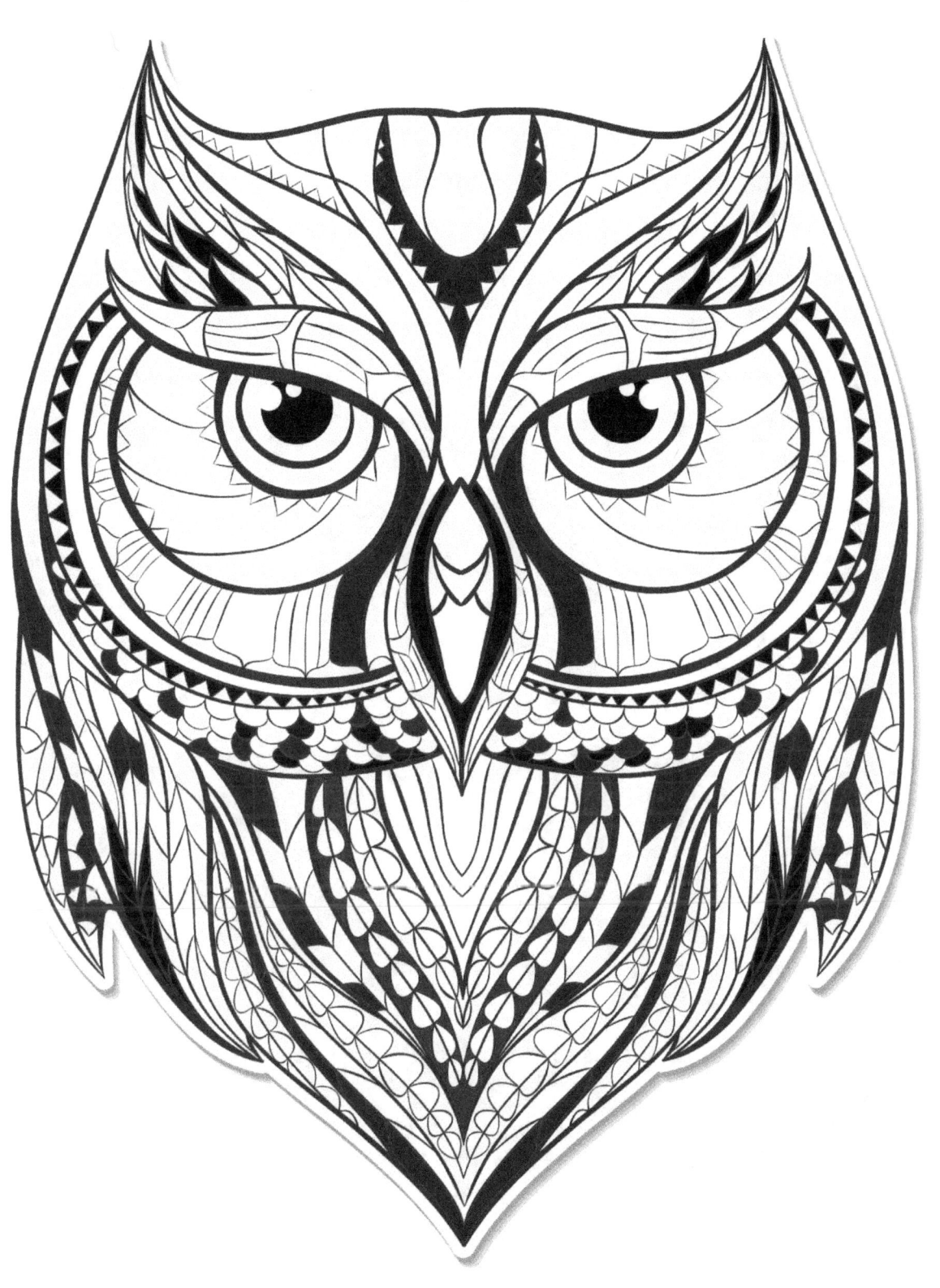

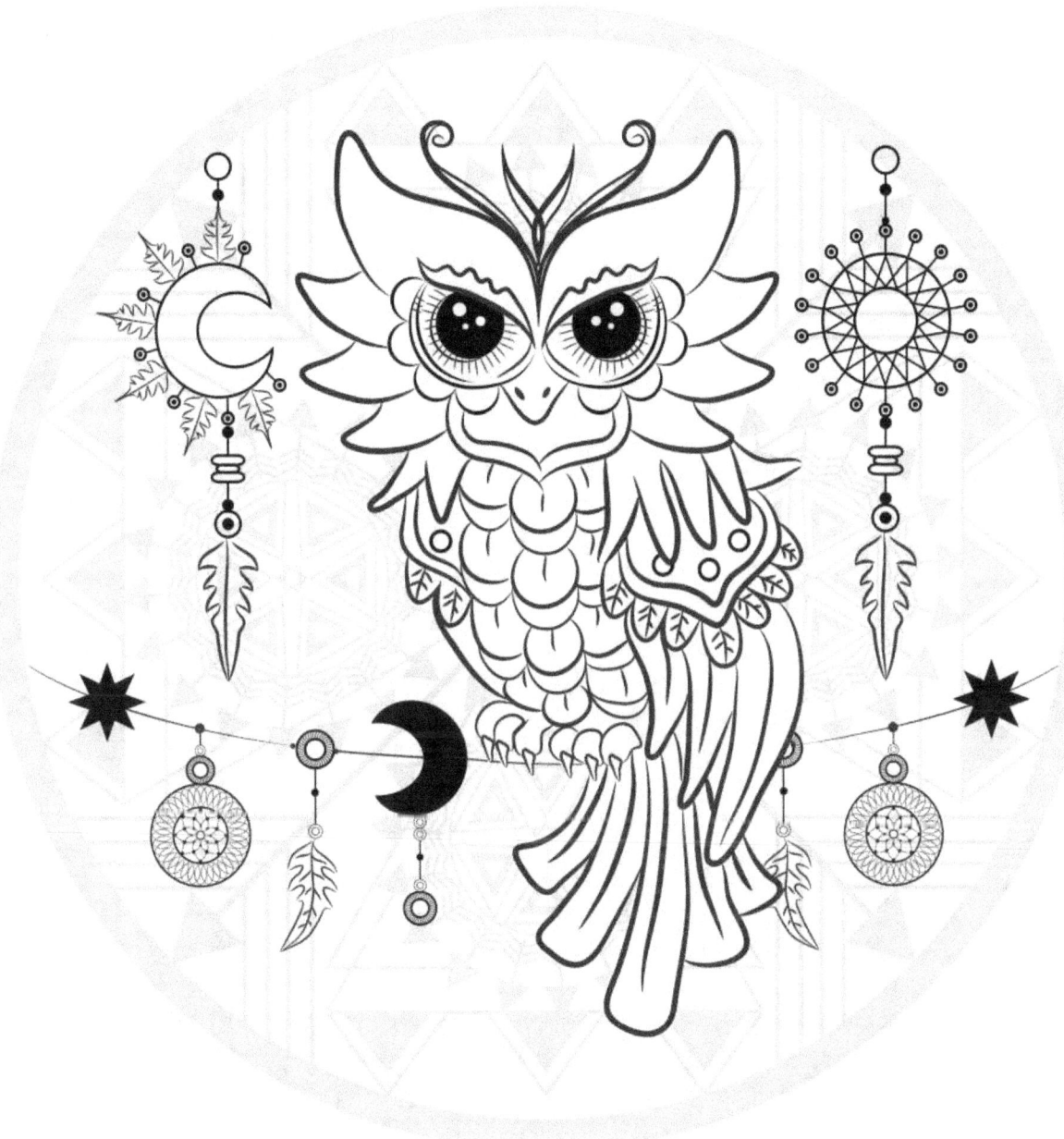

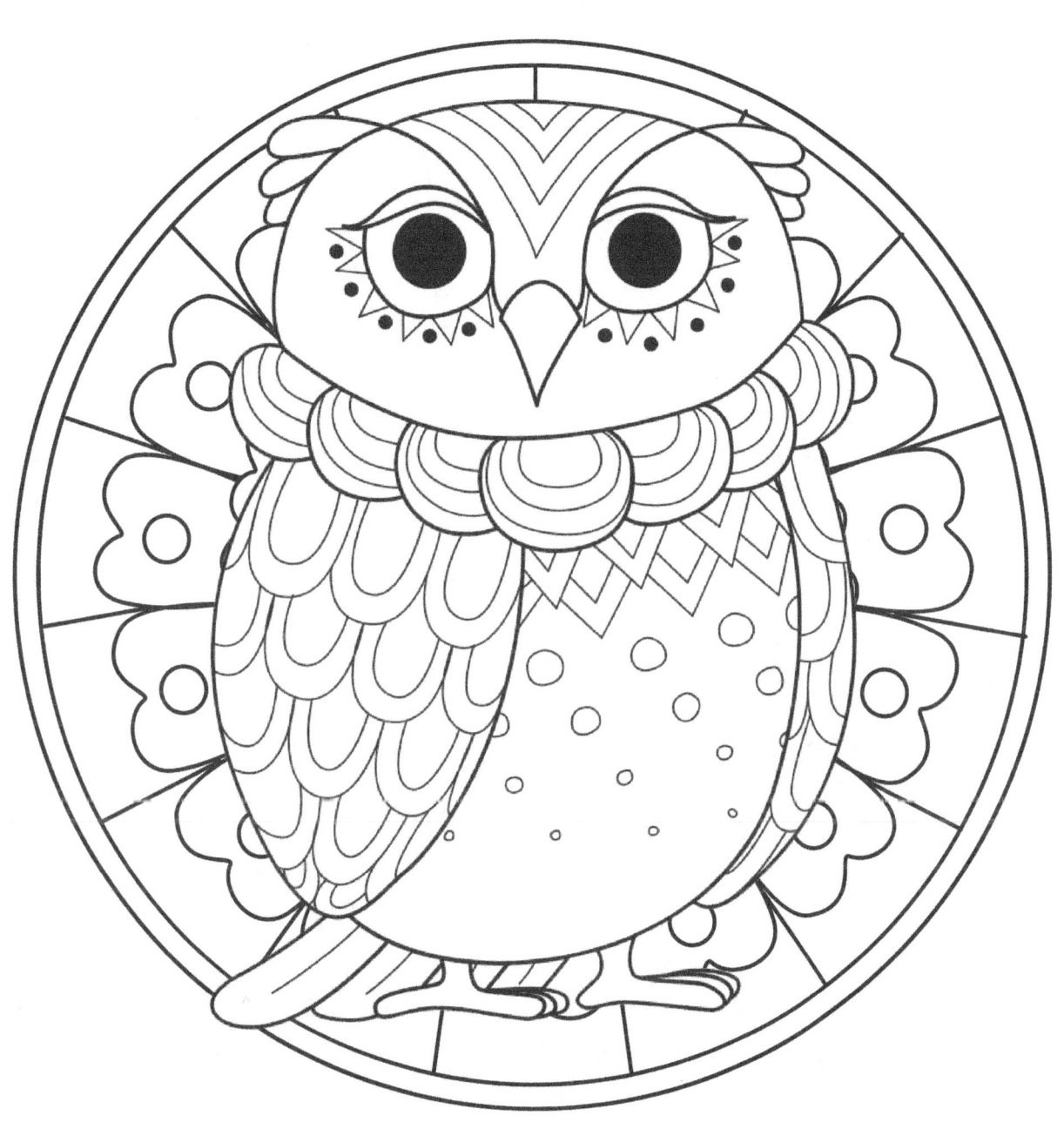

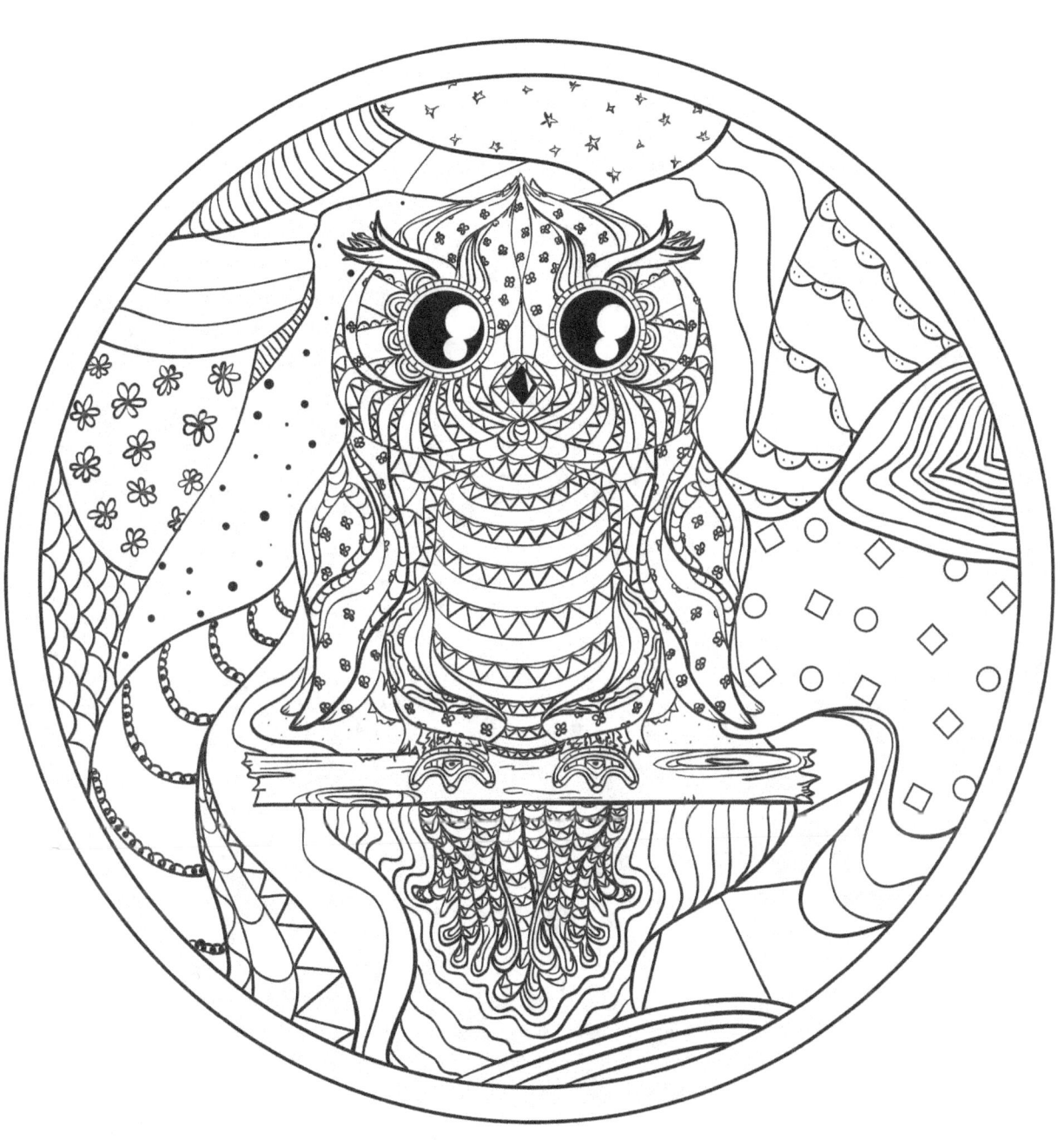

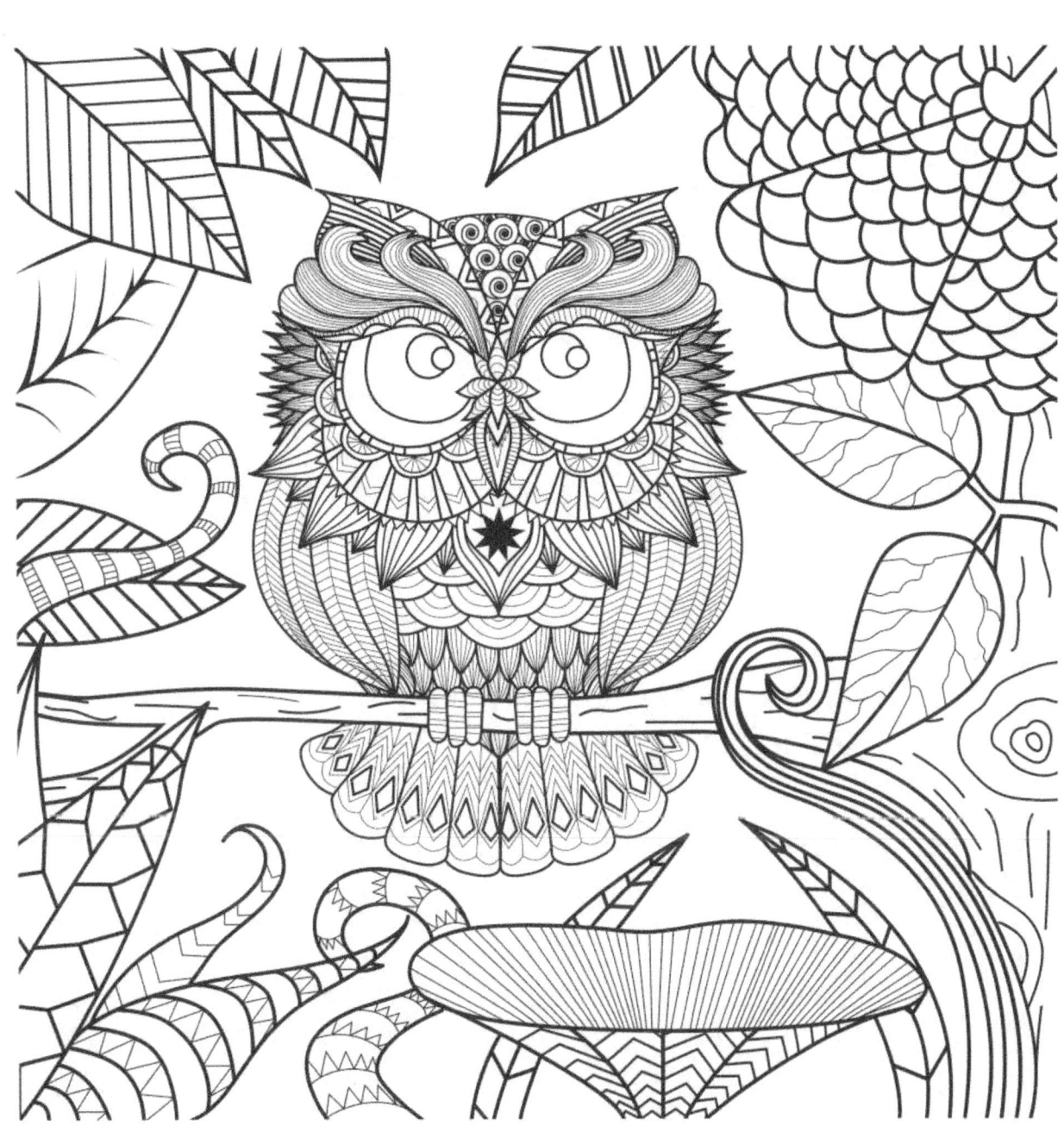

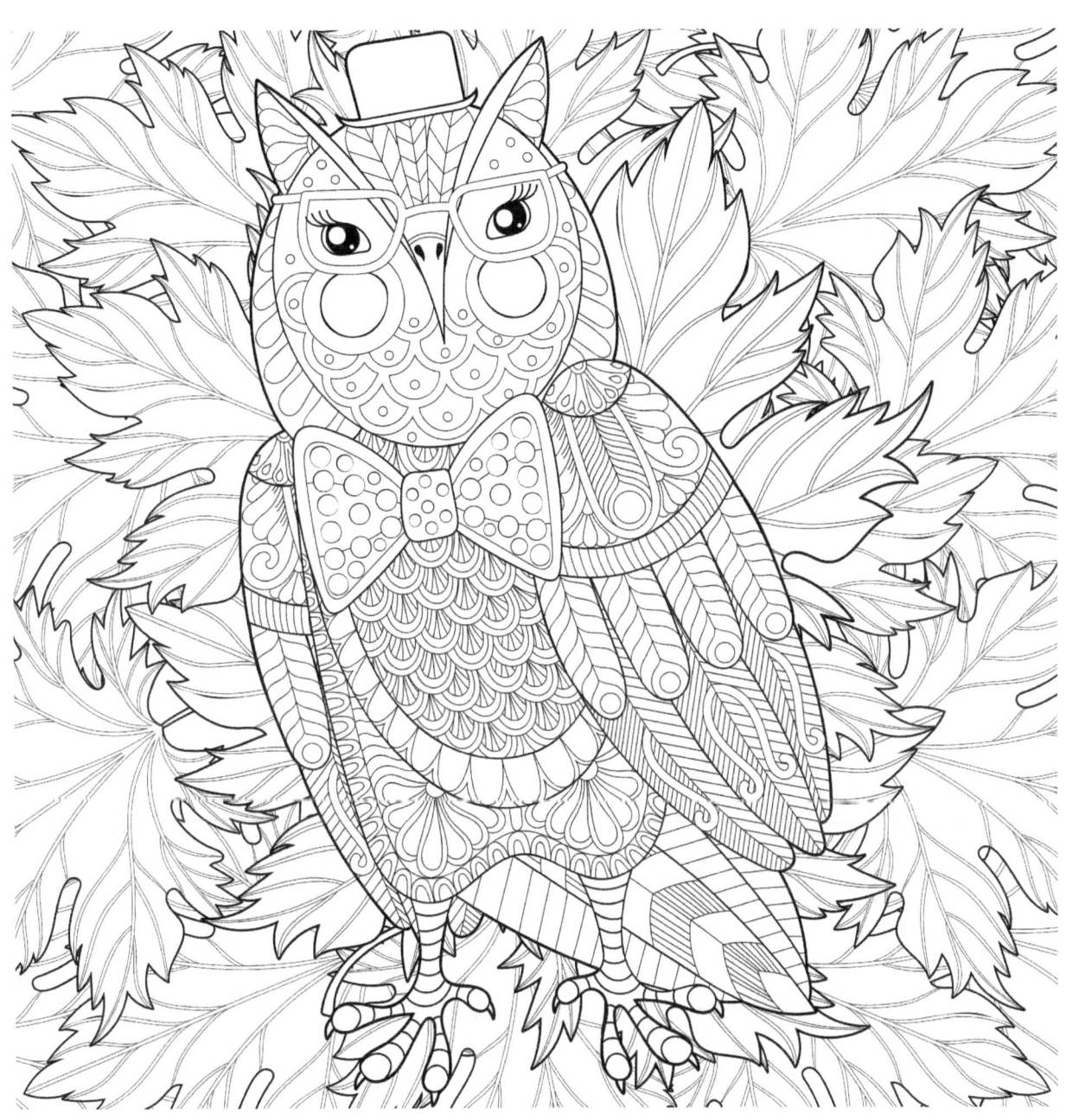

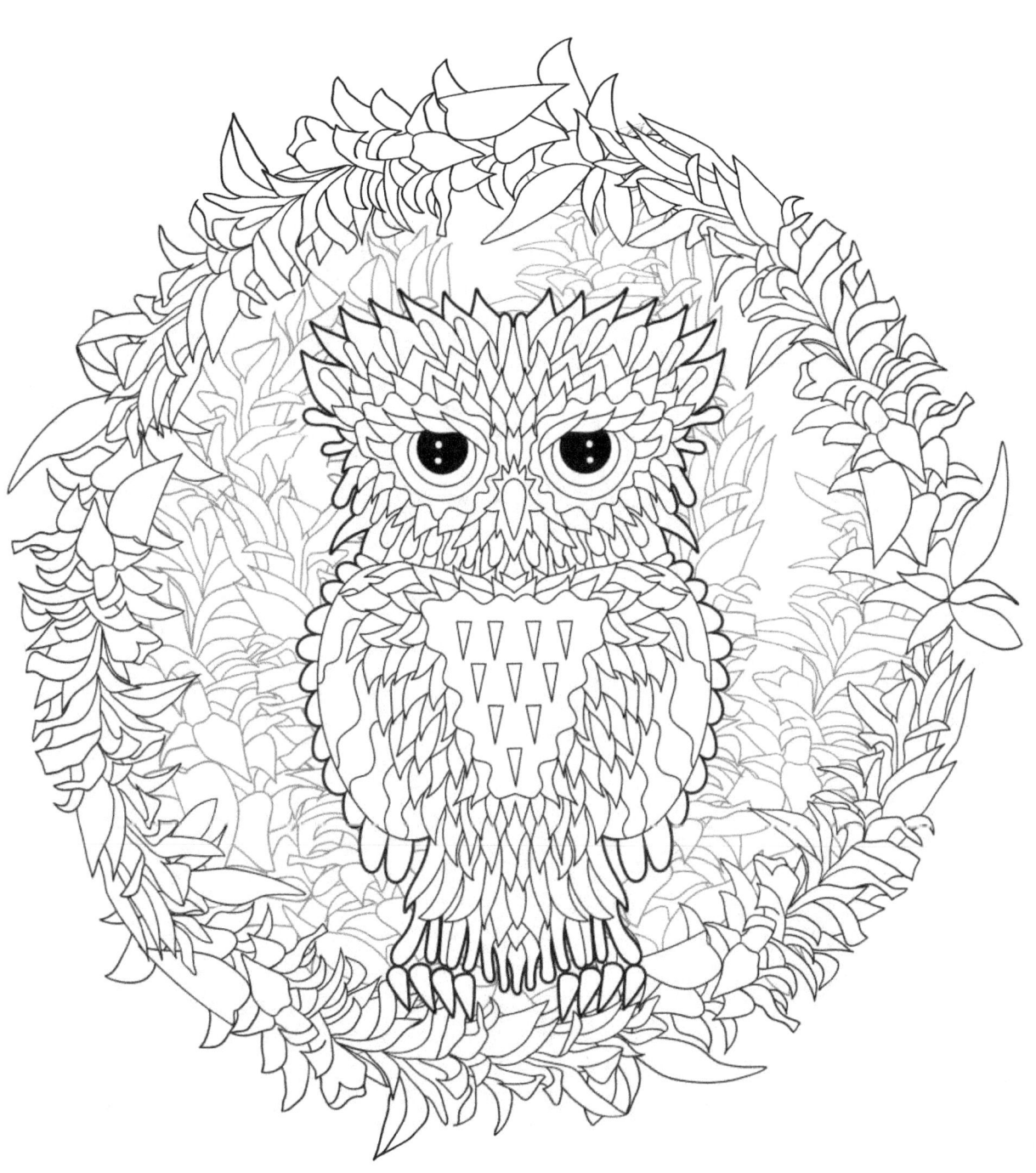

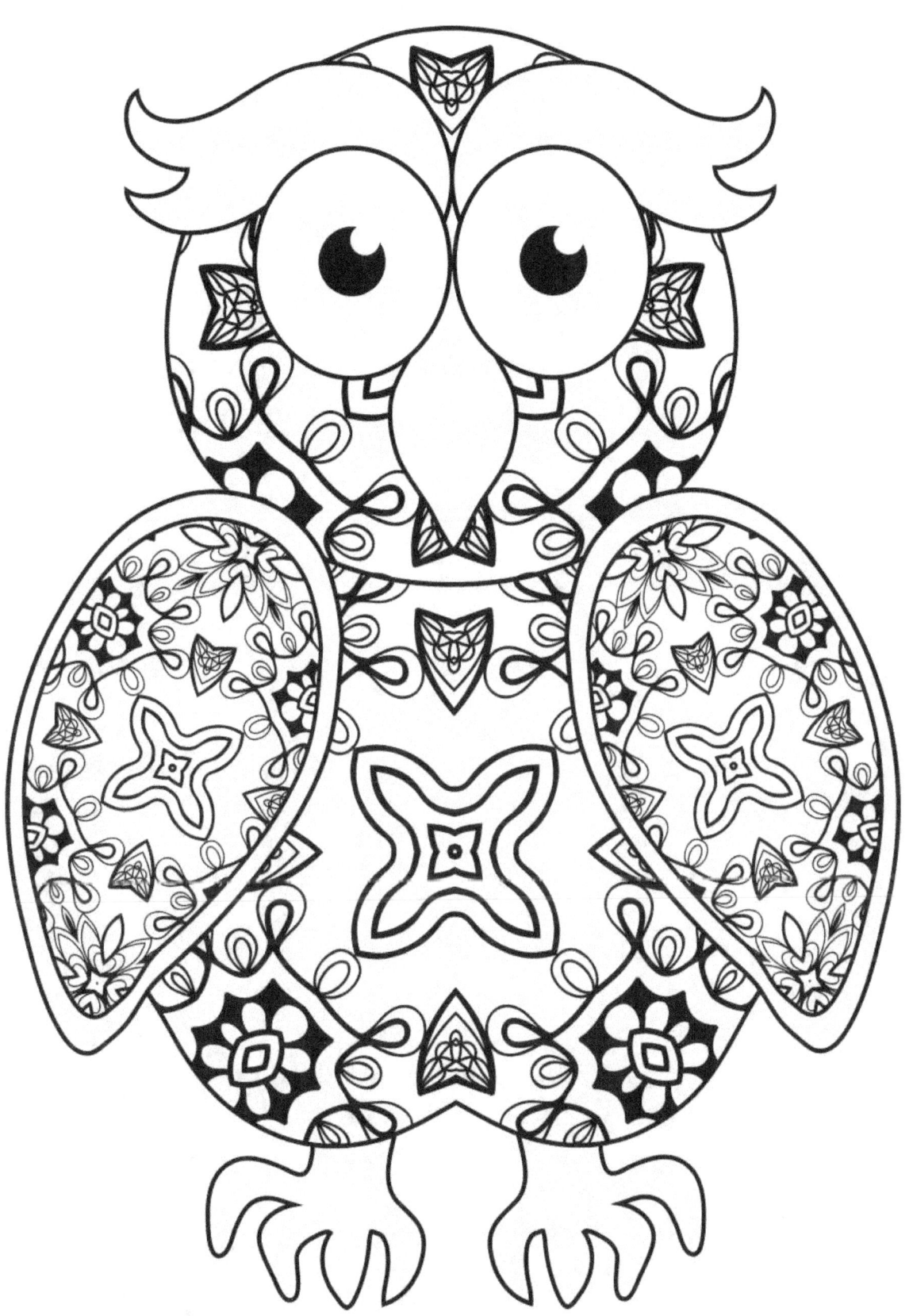

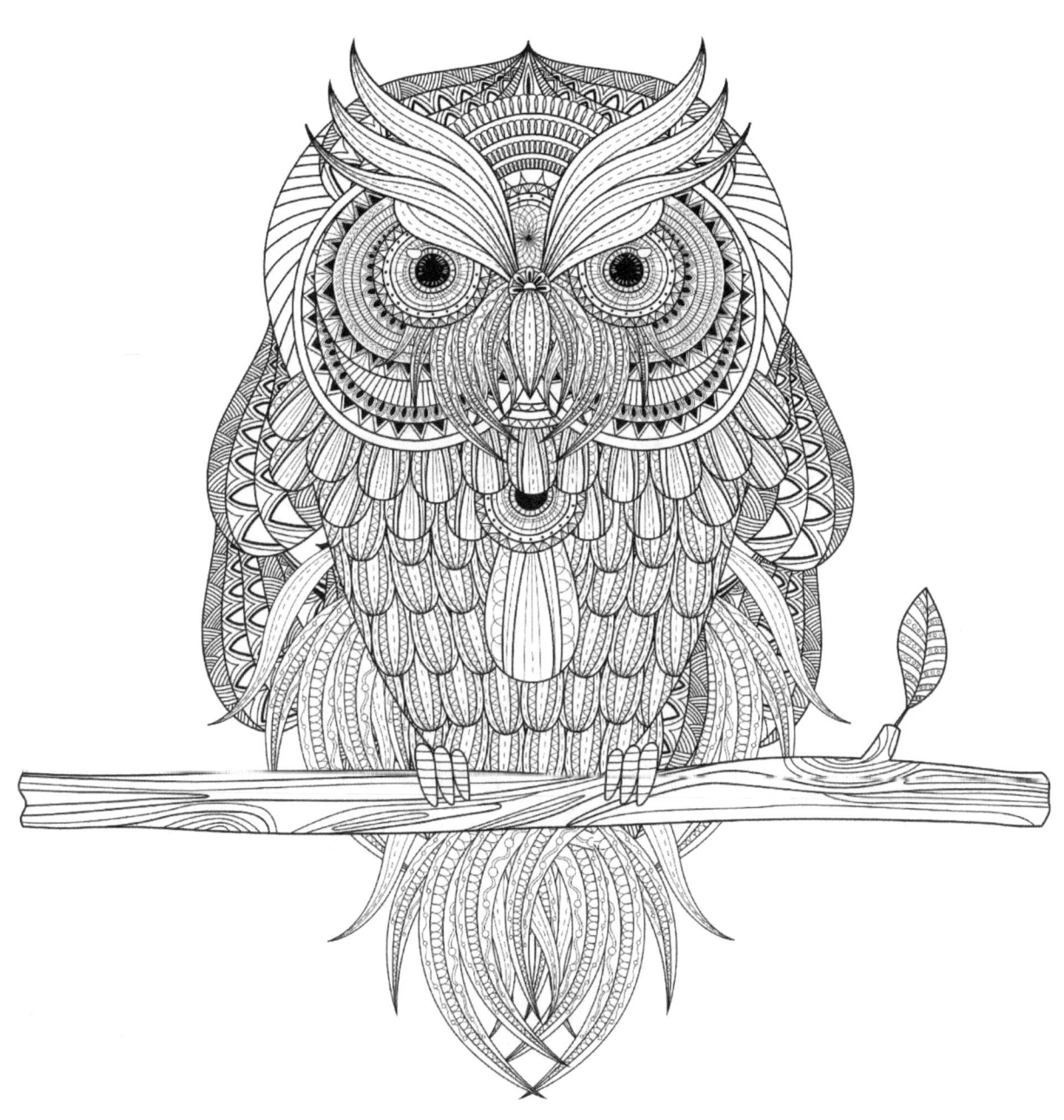

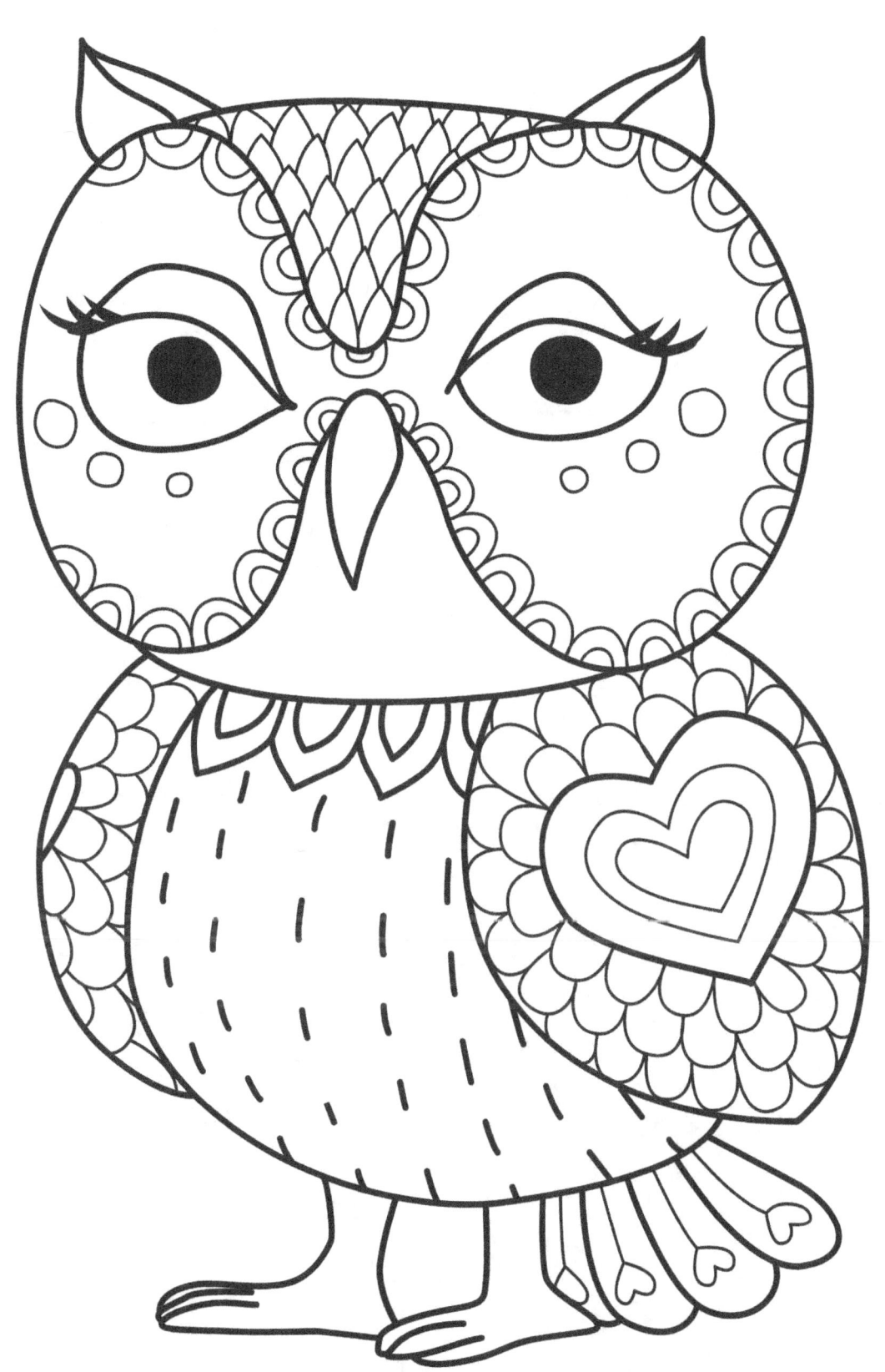

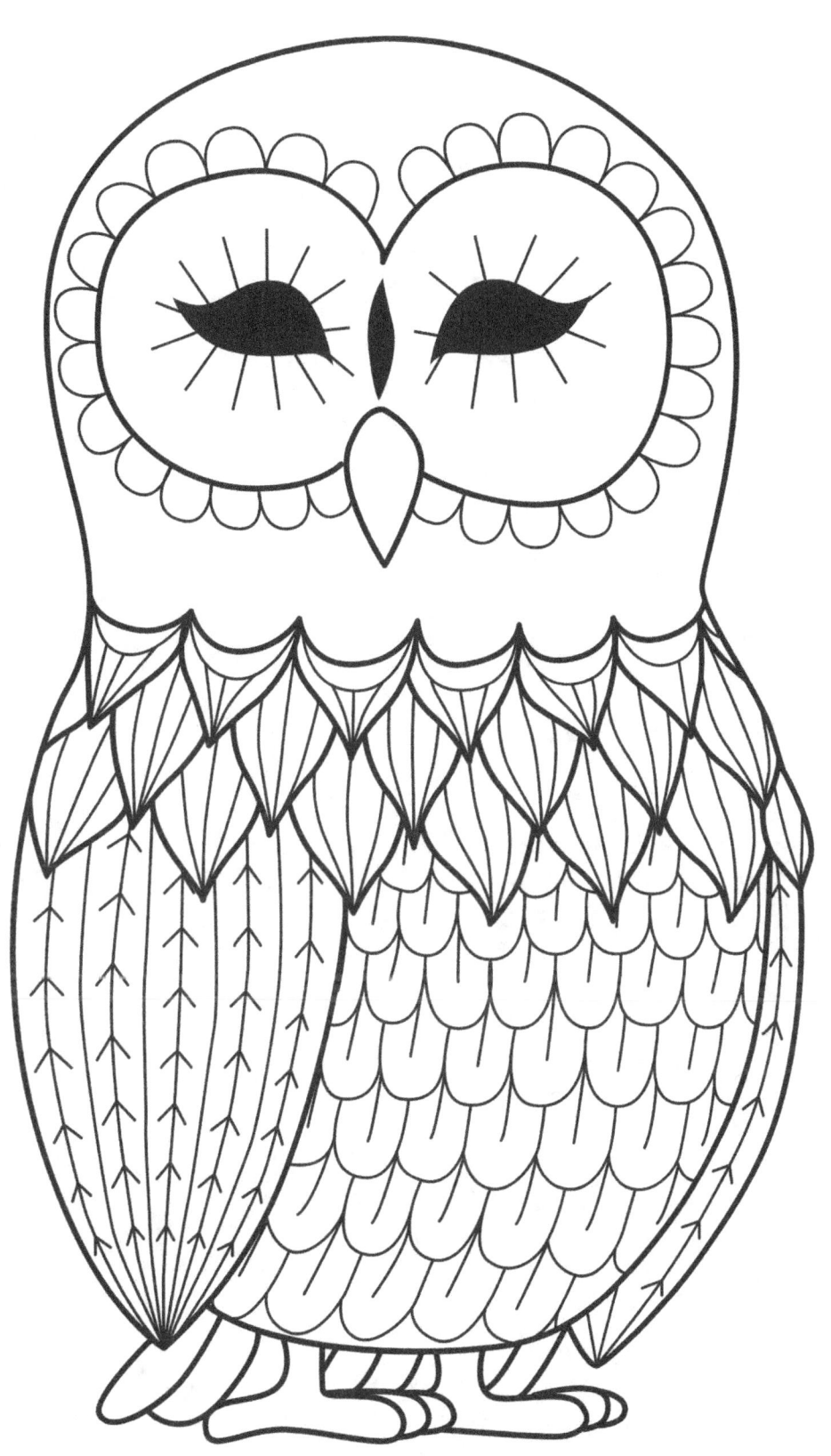

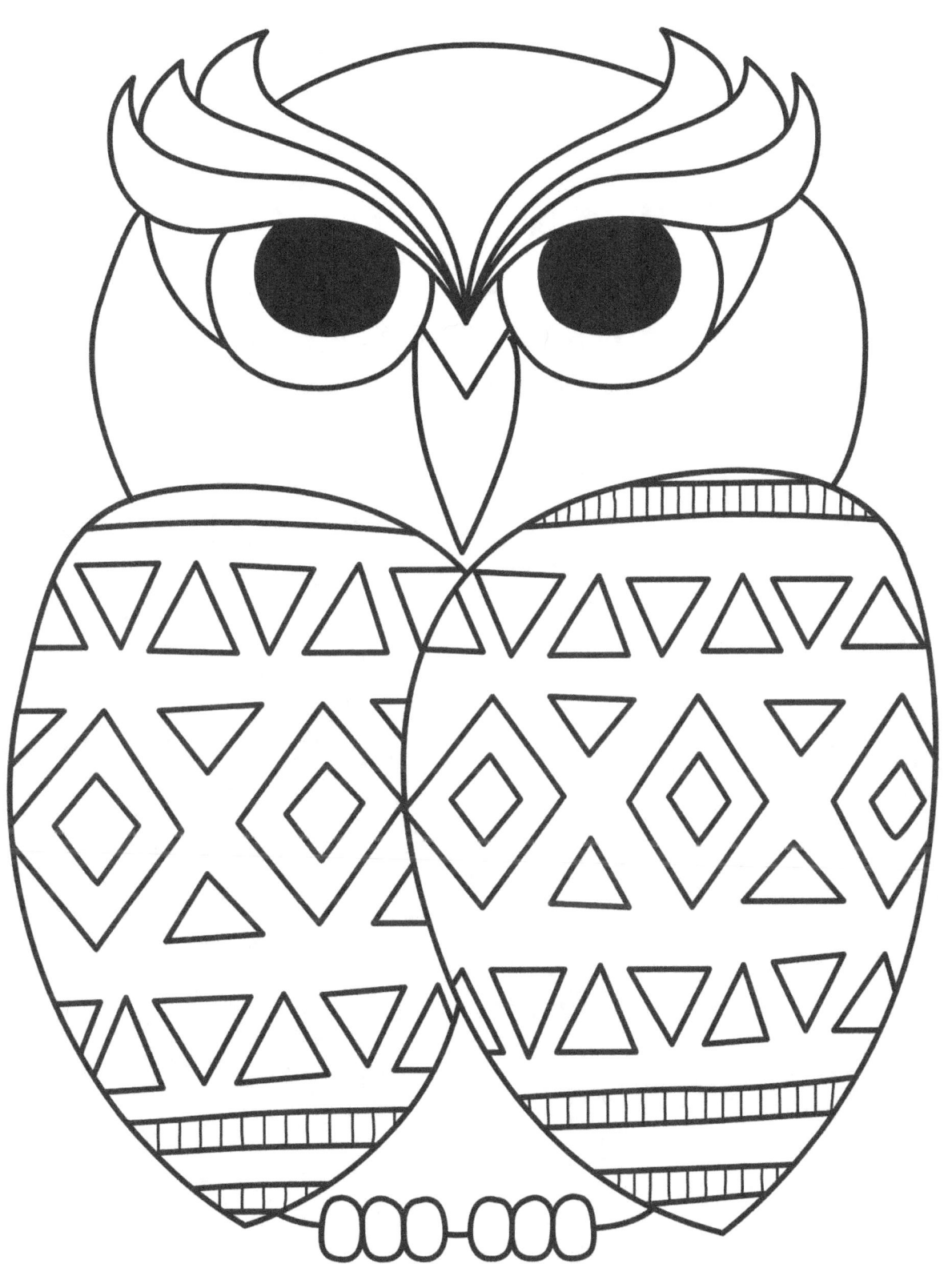

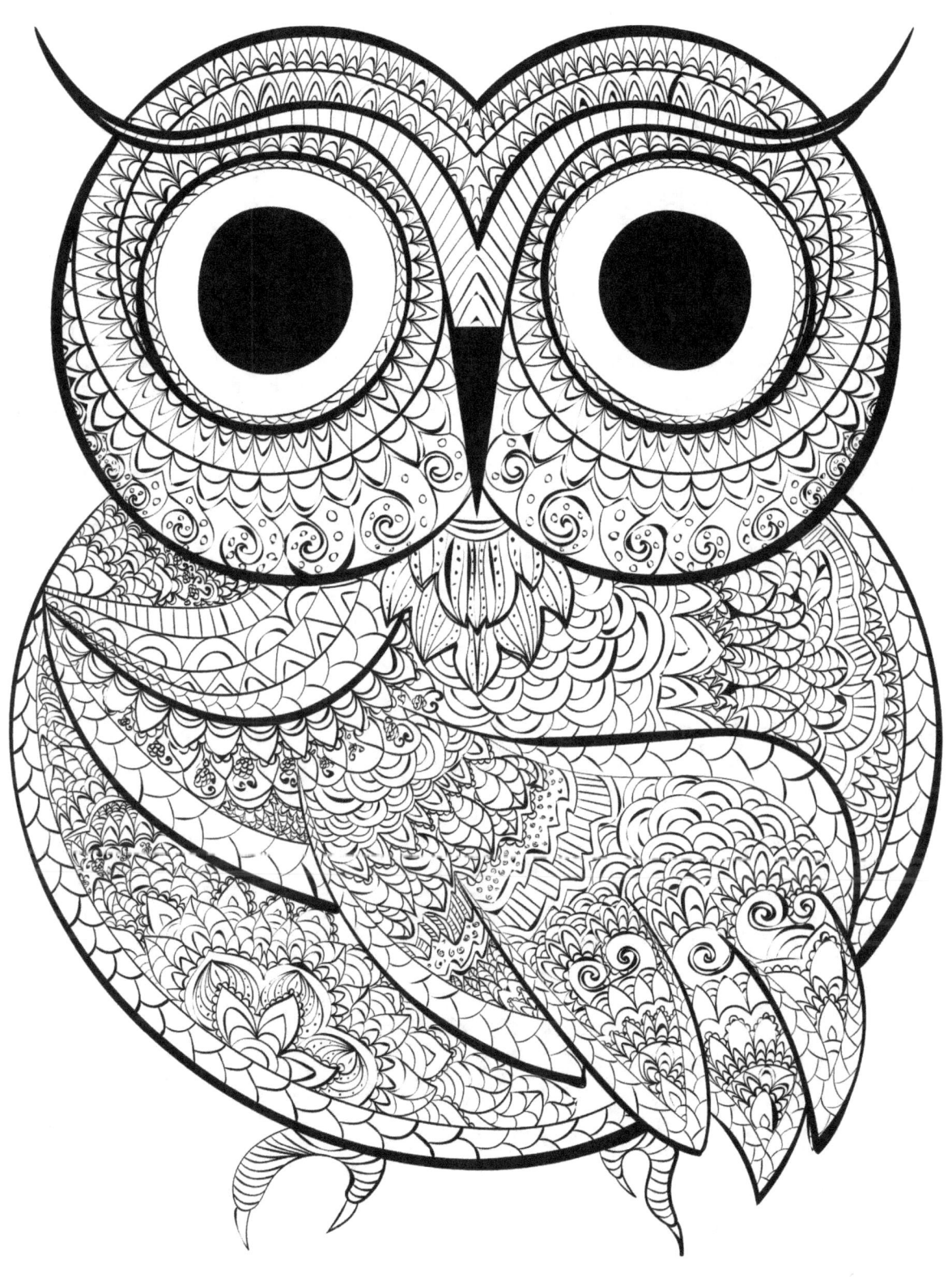

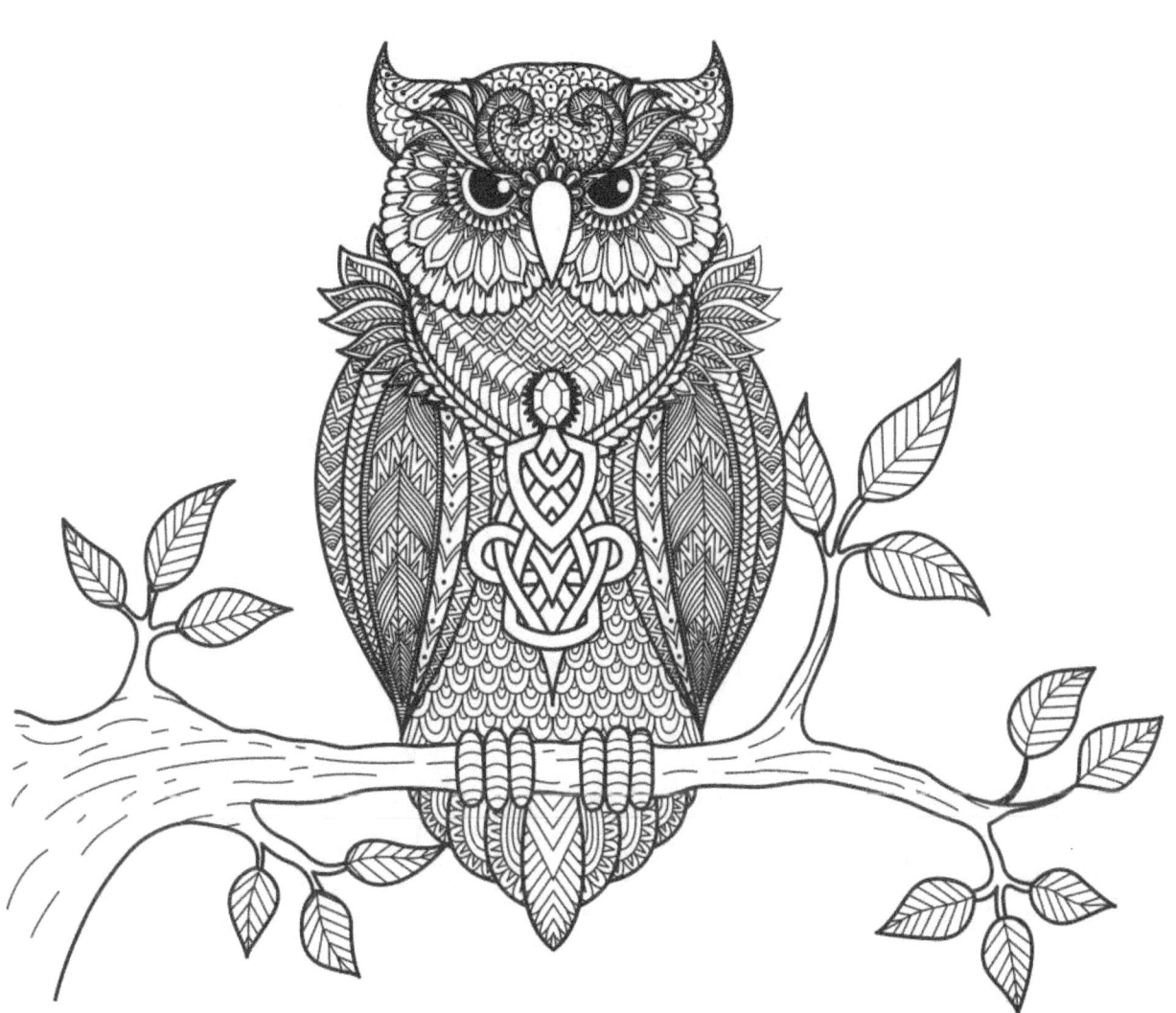

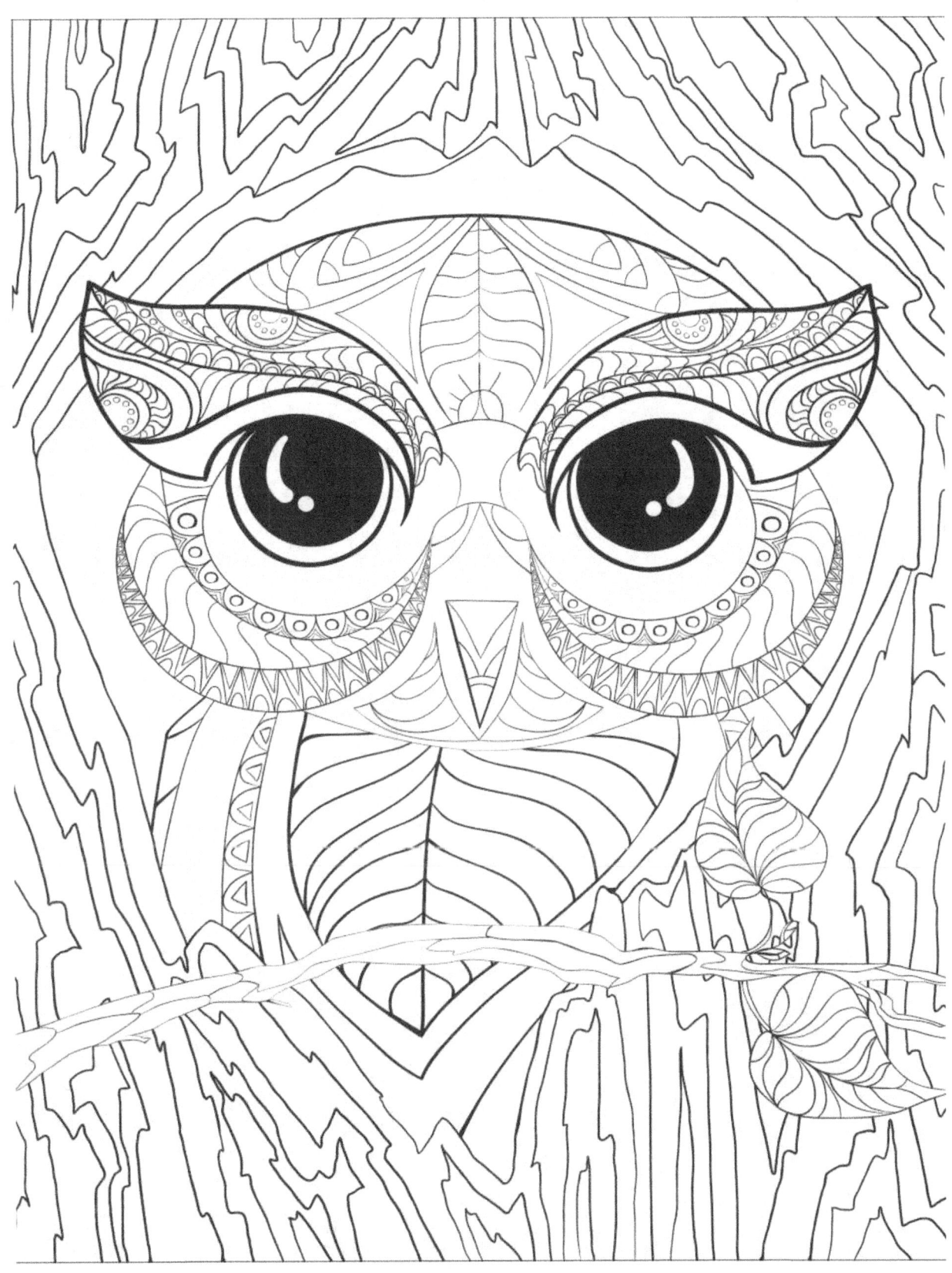

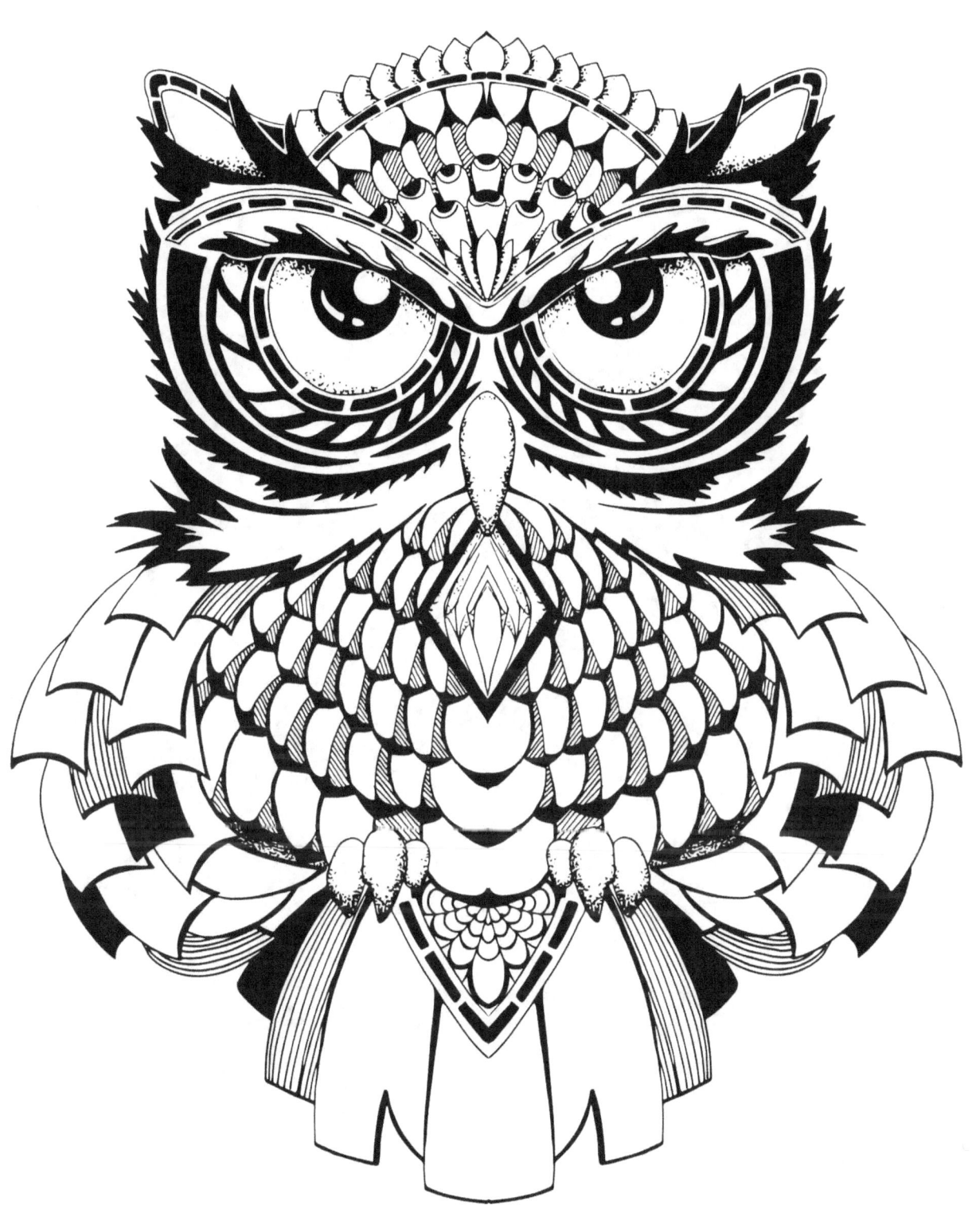

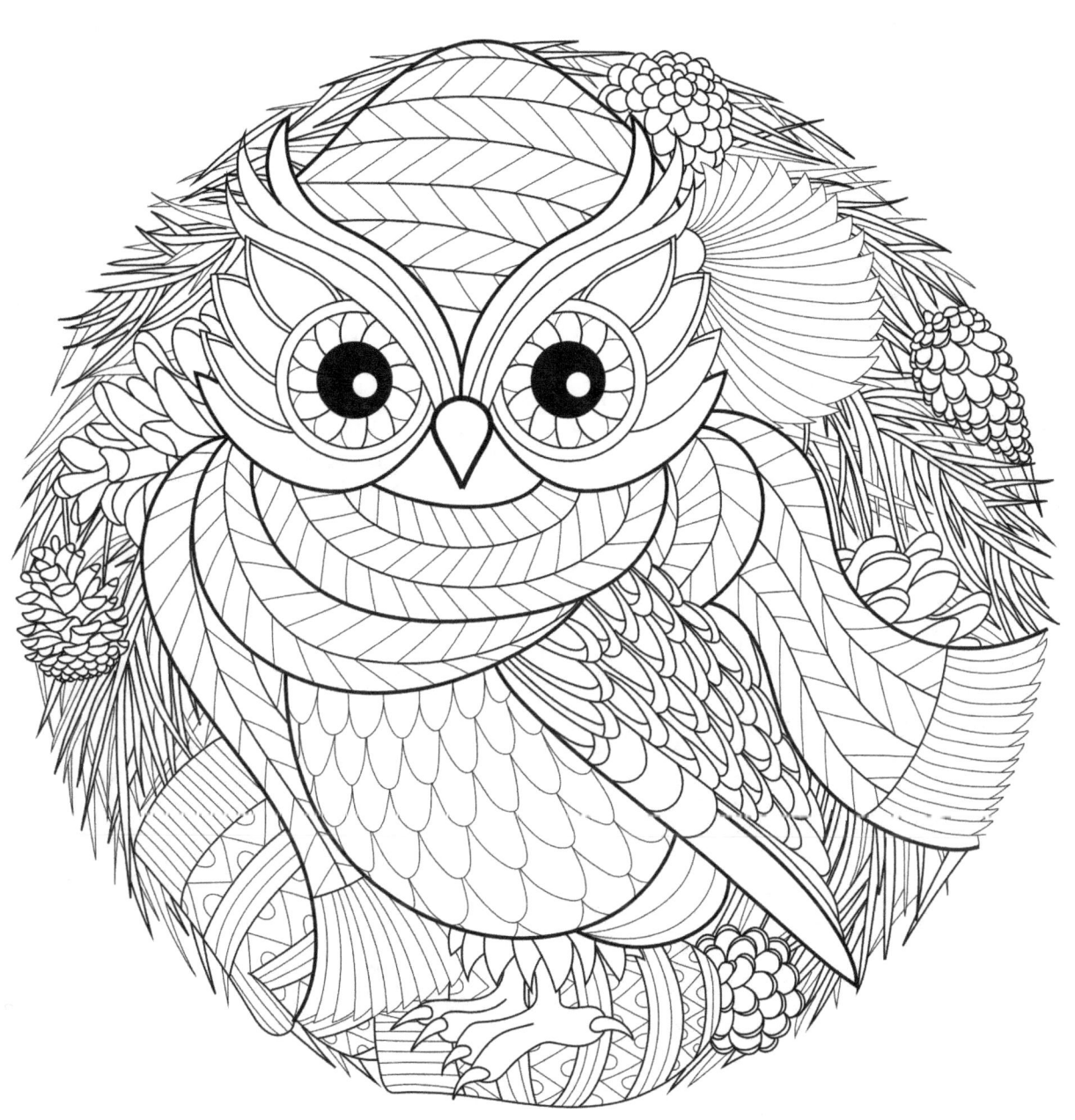

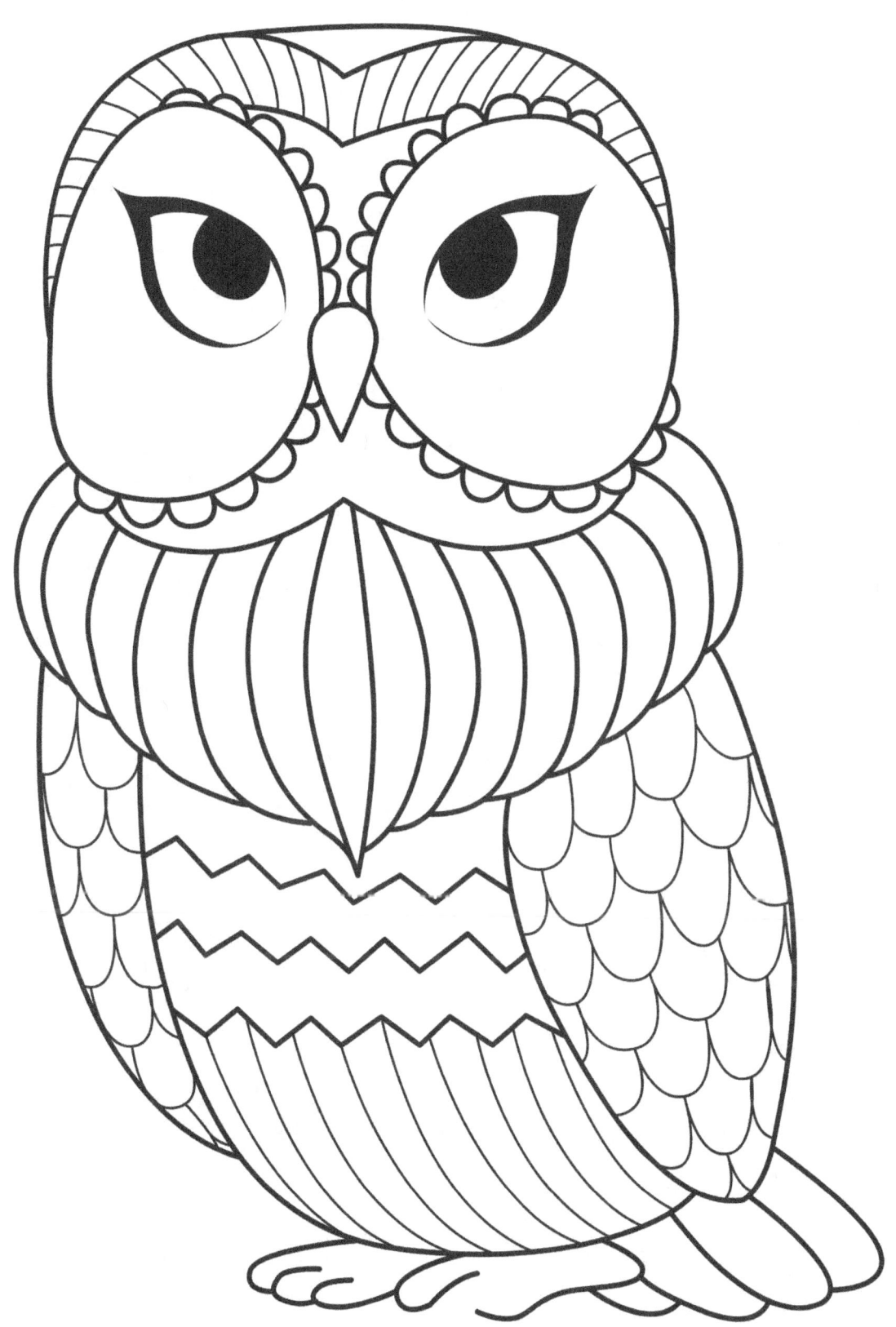

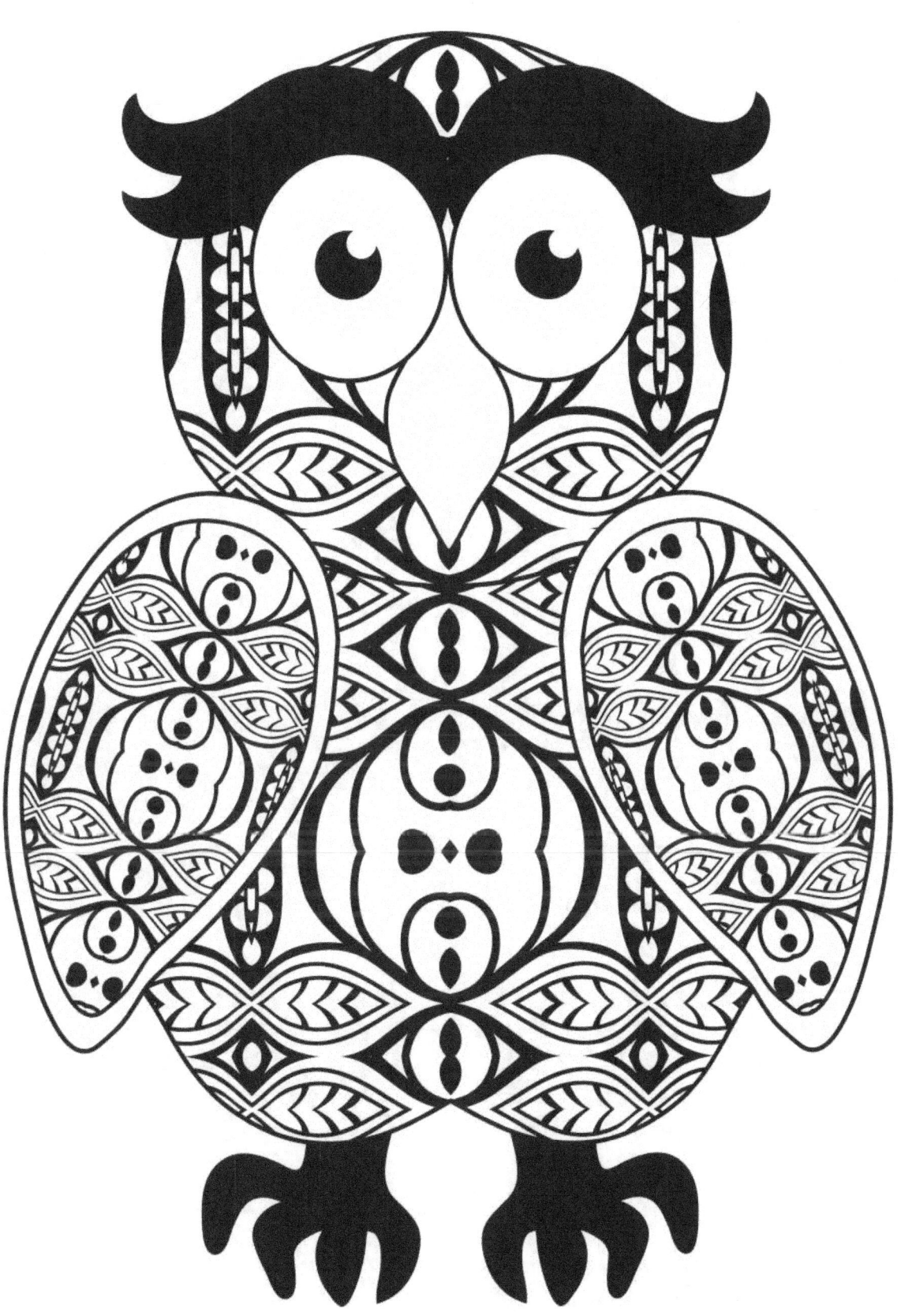

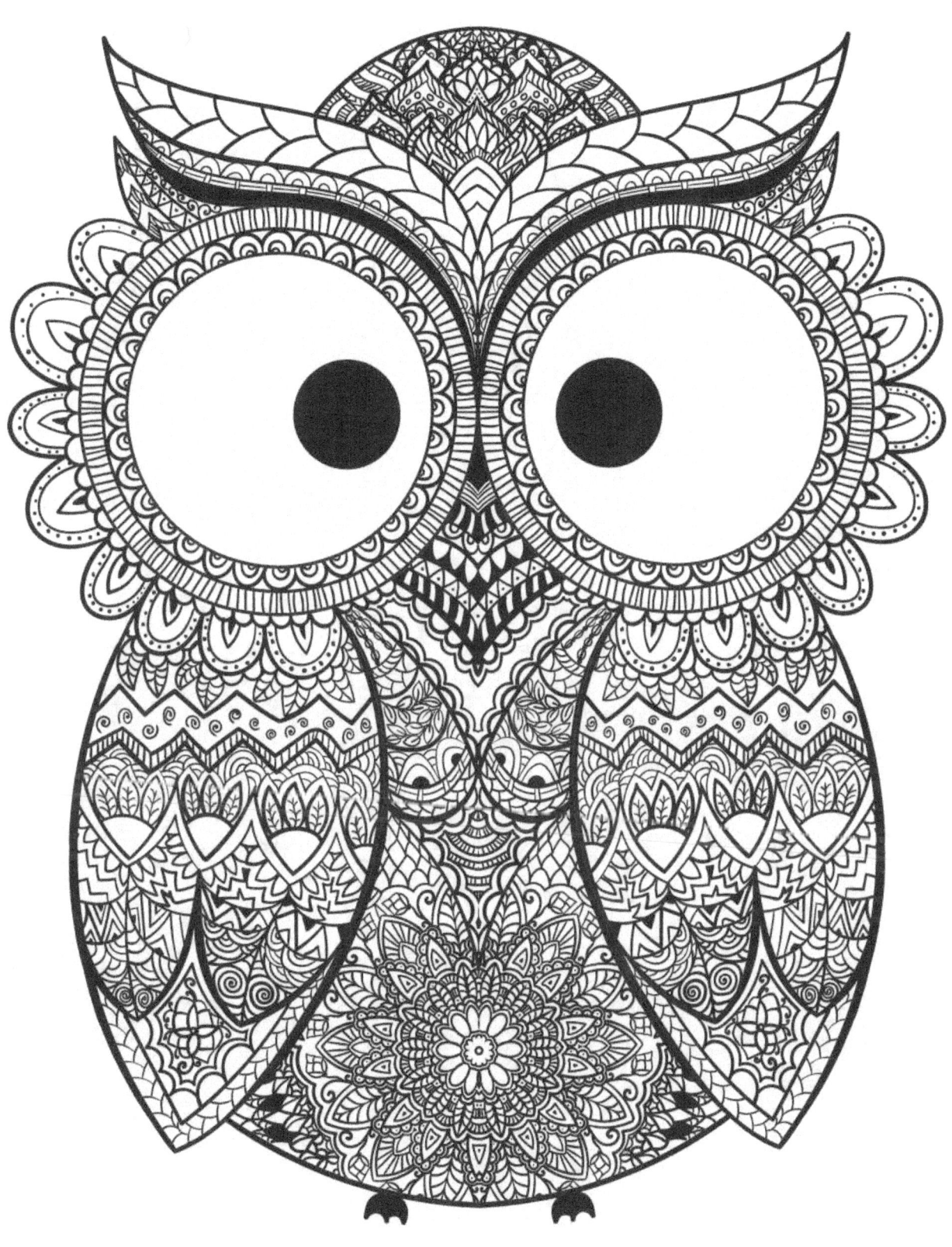

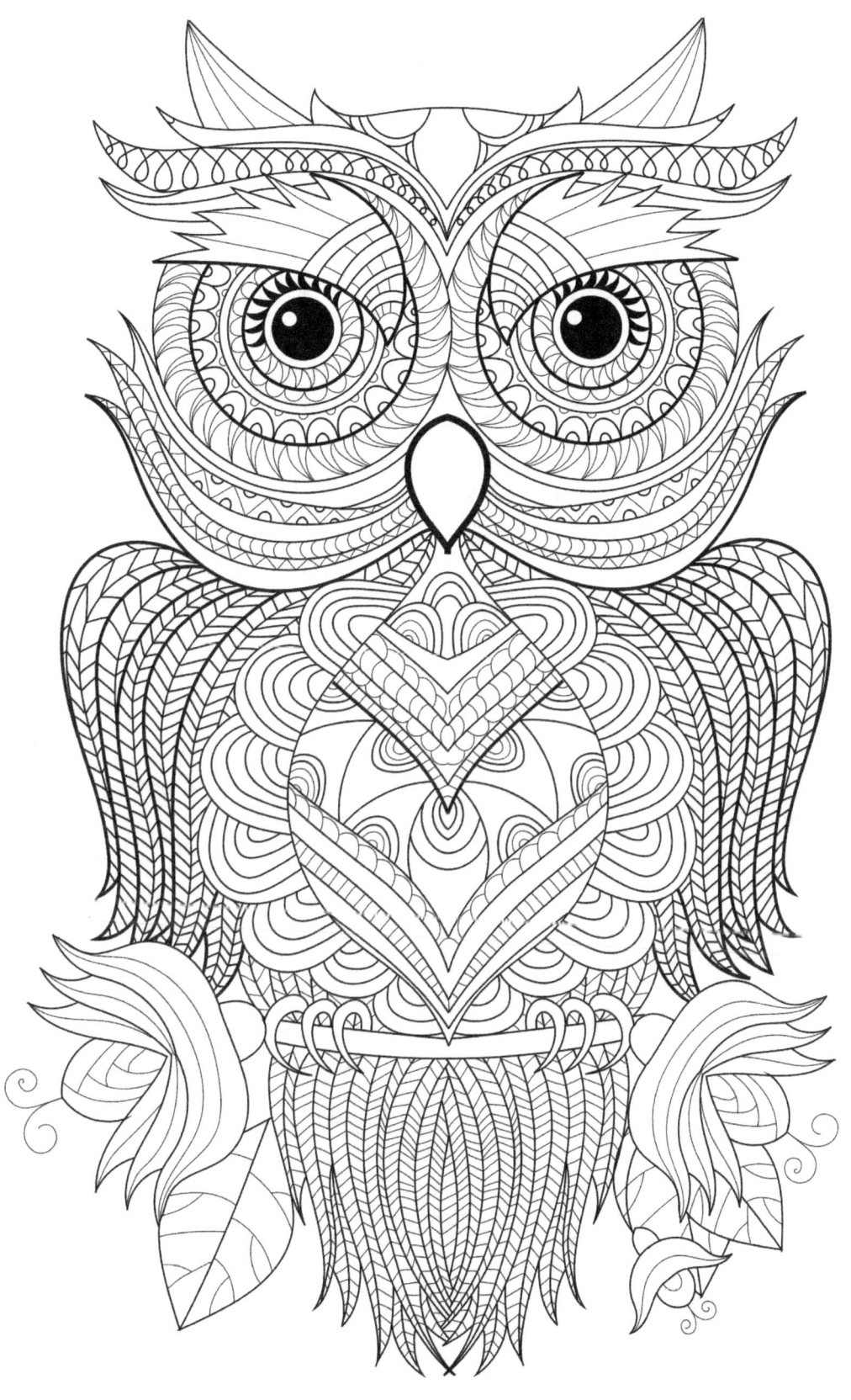

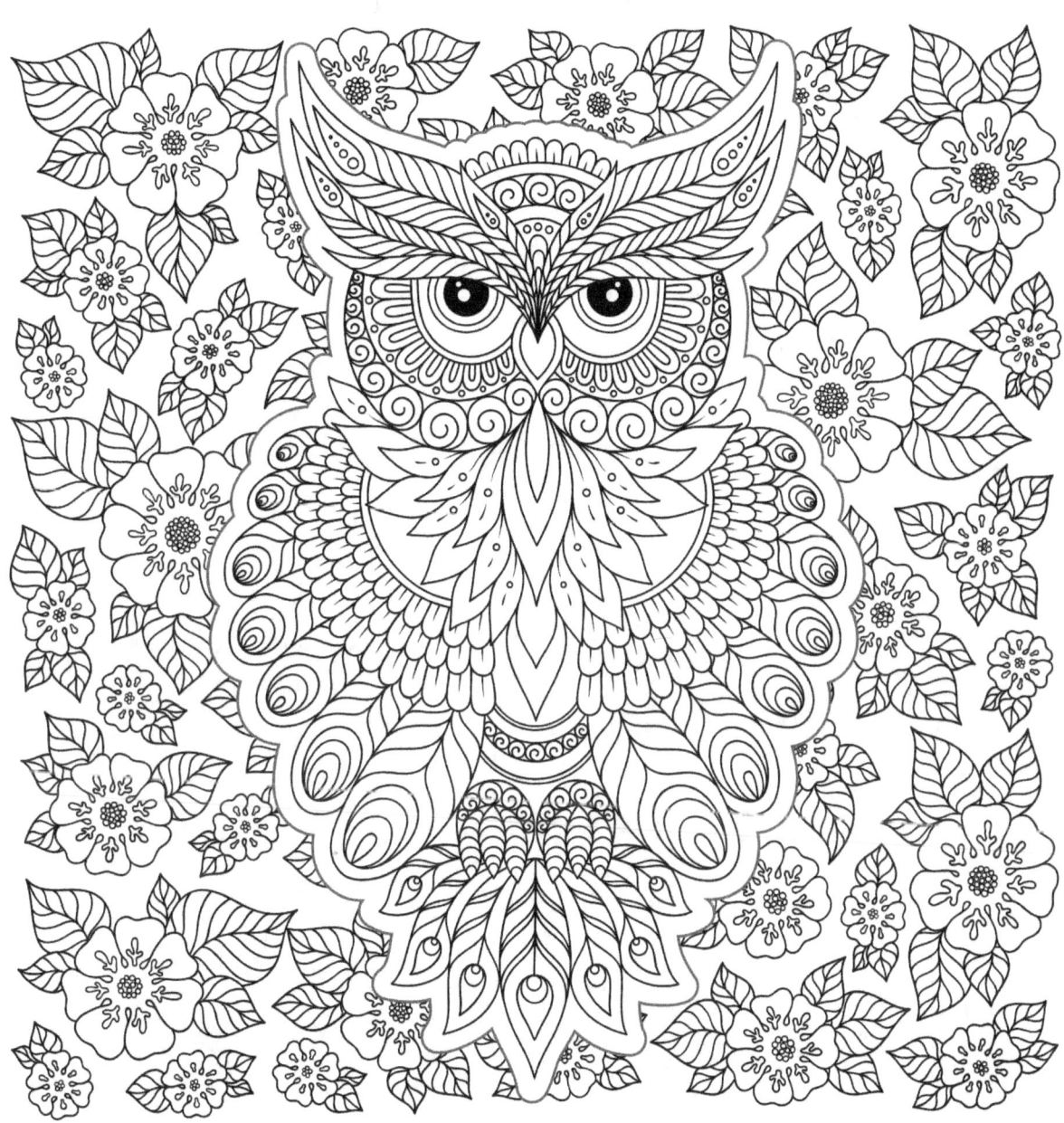

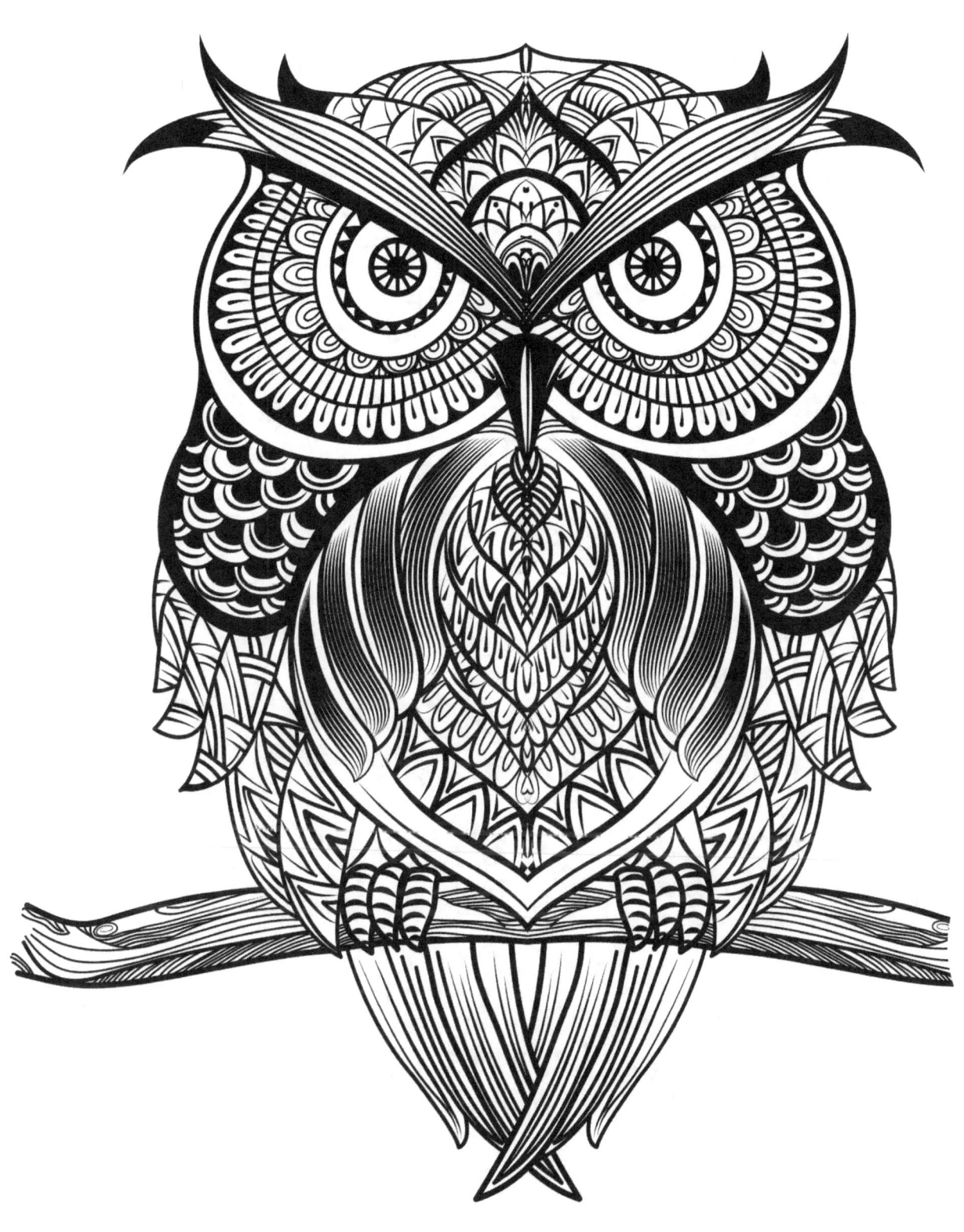

Amazing OWLS

Coloring Book

www.ingramcontent.com/pod-product-compliance
Lightning Source LLC
Chambersburg PA
CBHW080136240526

45468CB00009BA/2468